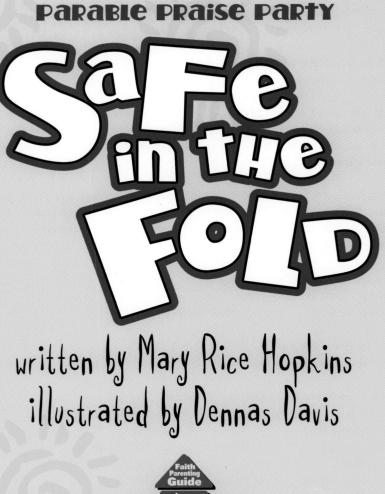

PARABLE PRAISE PARTY

Safe in the Fold

written by Mary Rice Hopkins

illustrated by Dennas Davis

Faith Parenting Guide

Ages **4-7**

Security

Faith Kidz®

A Faith Parenting Guide can be found on page 34.

Faith Kidz® is an imprint of Cook Communications Ministries
Colorado Springs, Colorado 80918
Cook Communications, Paris, Ontario
Kingsway Communications, Eastbourne, England

First printing, 2004
Printed in Korea
2 3 4 5 6 7 8 9 10 Printing/Year 08 07 06 05 04

Editor: Heather Gemmen
Interior Designer: Granite Design

Library of Congress Cataloging-in-Publication Data

Hopkins, Mary Rice.
  Safe in the fold / written by Mary Rice Hopkins ; illustrated by
Dennas Davis.
       p. cm. -- (Parable praise party)
Summary: A retelling in rhyme of the parable of the lost sheep. Includes
activities involving sight, sound, and touch.
  ISBN 0-7814-3989-2 (hardcover)
  1. Lost sheep (Parable)--Juvenile literature. 2. Bible stories,
English--N.T. Gospels. [1. Lost sheep (Parable) 2. Parables. 3. Bible
stories--N.T.] I. Davis, Dennas, ill. II. Title. III. Series.
  BT378.L6H66 2004
  226.8'09505--dc22
                            2003014775

To my Aunt Mabel for a love without limits
and boysenberry cobler. — MRH

For Valeria — DD

Once there was a farmer who had a hundred sheep. Every night he'd count them before he went to sleep.

But one day he was counting...one and two and thre
He saw that he was missing one.
"Oh, where could my lamb be?"

6

...ive and six and seven...up to ninety-nine.
"I will find my little lamb. I love him and he's mine."

The farmer kept on calling as he wandered far away.
He left the ninety-nine behind to find the one that day.

10

He searched by noisy rivers,
in the valley, by the creek.

He searched through dreary forests
and on the mountain peak.

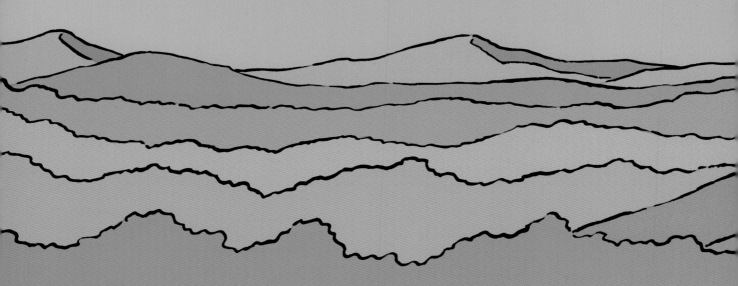

He looked beyond the meadow, in the field of wheat.
He often stopped to listen for a gentle, helpless bleat.

The farmer felt so sad to know his precious lamb was lost.
He said he would do anything no matter what the cost.

19

21

He scrambled down the hill, and then he made a giant leap.

23

The farmer saved the lamb, and with a smile on his face,
he carried his lamb to the fold where it was warm and safe.

There they had a party to celebrate the friend who had been lost but now was back to live with them again.

Jesus said,

"If a man owns a hundred sheep, and one of them wanders away, will he not leave the ninety-nine on the hills and go to look for the one that wandered off? And if he finds it, I tell you the truth, he is happier about that one sheep than about the ninety-nine that did not wander off.

In the same way your father in heaven is not willing that any of these little ones should be lost."

Matthew 18:12–14

Farmer and the Sheep

Words & Music by
Mary Rice Hopkins

1st verse

The far-mer is look-ing for his sheep He can't find___ him and
he can't sleep___ He looks high___ he looks low___ And he
looks to the moun-tains And the riv-ers be-low Oh

chorus

no he can't sleep___ Un-til he finds___ his lit-tle lost sheep Oh

31

Farmer and the Sheep

The farmer is looking for his sheep
He can't find him and he can't sleep
He looks high he looks low
And he looks to the mountains
and the rivers below

Chorus

Oh no he can't sleep
Until he finds his little lost sheep
Oh no he can't sleep
Until he finds his sheep
The sheep could be the only one
Through the briars through the meadows
He calls him to come
He looks up he looks down
And he keeps on looking until he is found

He can't sleep a wink
No he can't eat
Cause he missed
His little lost sheep
(repeat)

When he comes back to the fold
The farmer celebrates
with the young and old
He thanks God for he's found
He has a big party and invites the town

Second Chorus

Oh yea now he can sleep
But he wants to stay awake
and party with the sheep
Oh yea now he can sleep
But he wants to party with the sheep
(Repeat)

Celebrating with the sheep
He wants to party with the sheep

33

SAFE in THE FOLD

Ages: 4-7

Life Issue: I want my children to know how safe they are with God.

Spiritual Building Block: Security

Do the following sight activities to help your children understand God's care for them:

Sight: Gather your kids comfortably around you. Make sure everyone can see the pictures of the book. Read the story to your children. As you read, make gestures to show what is happening in the story: put your face on your hands to indicate sleep, count your fingers when the farmer is counting, hug yourself when the farmer says he loves his sheep, etc.

Point to the picture of the sheep on page 22 and ask your kids if they think the lamb wanted the farmer to find it. Point to the picture on page 26 and ask your kids if they think the farmer was glad to find it.

Tell your kids you are going to read the story again, but this time you want them to act it out. Hold the book up so they can see the pictures as you read, and make the same gestures you made the first time.

Tell your kids that we are like the little lost sheep (point to the sheep on page 22) when we don't love Jesus. Tell them that Jesus is like the farmer (point to the farmer on page 26) when we do love him. Jesus loves us so much, and he will always keep us safe.

Sound: Play the "Farmer and the Sheep" song. Sing together and follow along with the words. Tell your children to pay close attention to the words because afterward you are going to see how much they remember.

Ask your children why they think the farmer kept looking for the one little sheep when he had a whole flock back home. Talk about how the farmer must have loved that little sheep very much.

Start the song again, but this time stop the CD in the middle of the song. Have your children try to recall what the next phrase or word is. Do this a few times throughout the song. Congratulate your children when they get it right. When they don't know the words, encourage them by telling them that as they hear the song more often, they'll eventually remember.

Tell your kids that the farmer in this story is just like Jesus. Jesus loves all his children (point to each of your kids) so much he did a whole lot more than skin his knees: he died on the cross to forgive our sins. And, after he rose from the dead, he began a search for each of us so that he can take us home where it is safe and warm.

Touch: Create a treasure hunt in your children's bedrooms: hide items and then give clues so your children can find them.

The treasure (or hidden items) can be things like: a coupon that is redeemable for mint chocolate ice cream, an IOU for an outing to the new playground you drove past last week, a new book from the series your children can't stop talking about, socks with toes, etc. Come up with inexpensive gifts that will be true treasures to your children because they reflect your knowledge of the things they love.

The clues can be in various forms, but all of them will take your creativity.

1. Give instructions: Look under something that is soft (pillow). Stand at the doorway and then take three steps forward. Look on top of the thing in front of you (the dresser).

2. Provide a map.

3. Create riddles: I am a toy and the dog likes to play with me every day (a ball).

Each clue should lead to another location on the path toward the final treasure. In other words, give them the first clue, let that lead them to the pillow, and that to the dresser, and that to the ball until they finally arrive at the treasure.

As your children are enjoying their treasure, talk about how God treasures us so much, he will search in every and any place to find us if we ever stray from him. He will not quit looking until he finds us. Make sure your children understand that God does not lose us, but sometimes we lose him by paying attention to other things. God finds us by calling our attention back to him. We are safe with him.